A DAY IN THE LIFE OF A
Newspaper Reporter

by Martha T. Wickenden
Photography by Michael Plunkett and Larry French

Troll Associates

Library of Congress Cataloging-in-Publication Data

Wickenden, Martha.
   A day in the life of a newspaper reporter / by Martha Wickenden;
photography by Michael Plunkett and Larry French.
     p.   cm.
   Summary: Follows Yvette Ousley, a reporter for a large daily
newspaper, as she researches, interviews, observes in the field, and
writes her articles.
   ISBN 0-8167-2214-5 (lib. bdg.)   ISBN 0-8167-2215-3 (pbk.)
   1. Reporters and reporting—Juvenile literature. [1. Reporters
and reporting. 2. Occupations. 3. Ousley, Yvette.] I. Plunkett,
Michael, ill. II. French, Larry, ill. III. Title.
PN4797.W48 1991
070.4 '3—dc20   90-37547

The author and the publisher wish to thank The Times staff, especially Yvette Ousley,
Arnold Ropeik, Brian Malone, and Richard Bilotti, and wildlife biologist Tony Ross for
their generous assistance and cooperation.

Photography credits: P. 17, Tony Ross.

Yvette Ousley is a reporter with a large daily newspaper that serves readers throughout New Jersey and eastern Pennsylvania. She usually leaves her house around 10:00 A.M. and often doesn't return until late in the evening. On her way to work, Yvette buys today's editions of her paper— *The Times*—and several competing newspapers.

After a light breakfast in the cafeteria at *The Times* building, Yvette reads the newspapers she picked up. She checks to see if she has missed any stories that she should have covered or that she will want to follow up on today.

Before going to her desk, Yvette looks for some newspaper clippings in the *morgue*. A newspaper's morgue is a reference library of articles that appeared in previous editions of the paper. She checks to see what was reported about a fire that destroyed several homes in a nearby town. Yvette plans to do a story on the cause of the fire and how it might have been prevented.

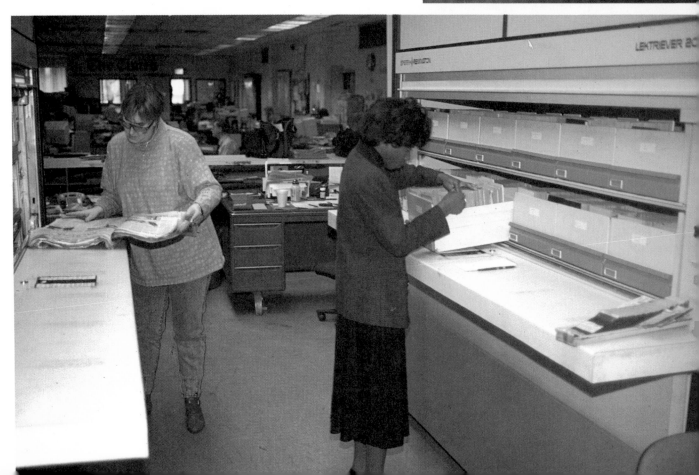

Yvette works in the newsroom, which is a large open area of desks arranged in rows. The room is filled with activity—reporters making telephone calls and writing their stories on video terminals at their desks, photographers picking up their assignments, and editors telling them what stories they should cover.

Today Yvette will follow up on the fire and other stories. She spends nearly an hour on the telephone, scheduling appointments with the manager of the town in which the fire took place, with an environmental engineer who runs a landfill, and with a wildlife biologist who is studying the habits of a deer herd in a nearby state park.

Before leaving the office for her interviews, Yvette talks with another reporter about her story on the fire, which probably will appear in the newspaper next week. She then checks a nearby bulletin board for copy deadlines and other notices. The story on the deer is for tomorrow's edition, and the deadline for completing it is 7:00 P.M. today.

At the town hall, Yvette checks her notes before going inside to interview the town manager about the fire. The town manager explains that the investigation centers around the fireplace chimney, where the fire originated. After the interview, he assigns one of the fire investigators to take Yvette to the site.

The investigator tells her that a fire in the fireplace had gotten out of control. It grew so large that it exceeded the safety recommendations of the fireplace manufacturer. He explains that the fireplace has been dismantled and taken to a laboratory for further tests. Yvette makes a note to call the laboratory.

Her next stop today is at a landfill, a large tract of land where solid wastes such as paper and garbage are disposed of. The disposal of waste is a subject in which many of the newspaper's readers are interested. Today she will gather background information for a future story. She interviews the landfill manager while watching the trucks enter and leave the site.

Waste management, or the safe disposal or recycling of trash, is a highly technical science. Engineers and environmental scientists plan and operate the landfill, making sure that the waste does not pollute the air, soil, or water. Yvette visits one of the large areas that is being filled. Waste is hauled to the site in big trailers from cities and in smaller trucks from nearby towns.

The bottom of each dumping area is lined with plastic, which holds the rainwater that drains to the bottom. Pumps are lowered through large pipes. The water is then pumped to a filtration plant, where it is cleaned. Yvette interviews a workman who is building a cement house around the pipes. Like Yvette, he is wearing a safety helmet for protection against accidents.

Yvette's next appointment is in the soggy fields of Tyler State Park. She slips on her boots while waiting for the wildlife biologist and his assistant to arrive. They show her an antenna and a radio receiver that are used to keep track of deer living in the park. Radio signals are picked up from battery-operated transmitters attached to collars around the deer's necks.

The wildlife biologist locates a doe hiding in the thickets nearby. It has lived here since its birth less than two years ago. Yvette learns that a deer usually stays within two or three miles of its birthplace. When necessary, however, deer will travel up to seven or eight miles to find food or adequate cover. Cover for a deer means a heavily wooded area that provides easy concealment.

When some deer suddenly run across the field, Yvette spots the doe with the collar. The collars are wrapped with a bright yellow tape, which makes the deer easier to see in the wild. The radio frequency number is marked on the inside of the collar. A soft rubber tube covers the antenna to protect it.

To attach the collars, the deer are first
tranquilized, or put to sleep. The collar is adjusted
to fit snugly, so the deer will not snag it on a tree
branch or catch one of its front legs in it while
leaping or running. Although the collar is not
harmful, it feels strange at first. However, the deer
gets used to it very quickly.

Yvette usually covers news stories in her own semi-rural news beat, or assigned area. However, she is sometimes given special assignments in the city. For example, after a new governor was elected, Yvette was assigned to cover the swearing-in ceremony. Although the setting was different, her duties were the same—gathering the facts and reporting the news.

A large number of people had gathered at the state capital to watch the governor take his oath of office. There were dozens of reporters from television, radio, and the newspaper, as well as many government officials, some of whom made speeches. Yvette took notes that she later referred to when writing her story about the events.

A parade was to follow the speeches, so Yvette interviewed a member of a high school marching band, as well as a group of students dressed in colorful costumes from around the world. They were so nervous about marching in the parade that Yvette arranged for one of the photographers from her newspaper to take their photographs for a human interest story.

Yvette walked up and down the parade route, gathering the reactions of the spectators. She stopped to talk to a group of elementary school students who had been given the afternoon off to attend the parade. This was their first inaugural parade, and they were excited about getting a glimpse of the new governor.

As the marchers passed by, Yvette recognized some of the youngsters she had interviewed earlier, and she noticed that they did not look as nervous as before. In fact, some of them seemed to be having as much fun as the spectators. Before leaving the parade, Yvette called her editor to see if there was anything else she should cover before heading back to the office to write up her story.

Although not as much fun as a parade, the stories that Yvette covers on her regular beat are usually just as important. Soon after leaving the state park, Yvette pulls into *The Times* parking lot. She must finish writing her story about the deer and file it with her editor by 7:00 P.M. Since it's already five o'clock, she stops in the cafeteria to pick up a quick meal to eat at her desk while she works.

Yvette confers with her editor about the story. He suggests adding some new statistics, and Yvette makes a call to gather them. It's the editor's job to make sure every news story is thorough and *balanced*. A balanced news story or article contains comments from people on both sides of the issue.

The editor tells Yvette that her story should fill a 15-inch column in the newspaper, the maximum length of any story that appears on an inside page. This means that she will have to write at least 600 words. If Yvette's story is too long, it must be cut to fit the allotted space.

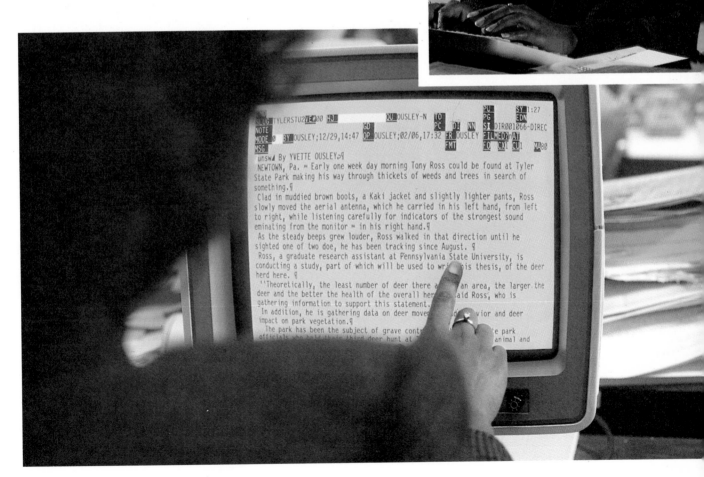

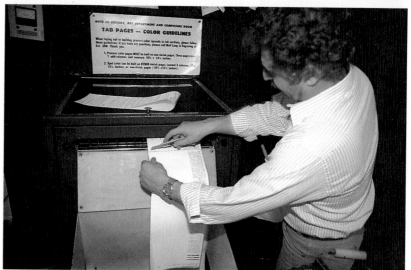

When the story is completed, it is checked again and assigned to a copy editor, who checks it for any grammatical or spelling errors and writes a headline. Yvette's story is then electronically sent to a computerized typesetter—a machine that automatically sets the type in columns on photographic paper.

Yvette's story—now on the photographic paper—is treated with wax on one side and pasted down onto sheets of lightweight, white cardboard. These are called "boards," and there is one for each page of the next day's newspaper. Using a razor blade, the "paste-up" person cuts and fits the story into its correct position. On some newspapers, this is done electronically on computers.

The board is then made into a negative image, just like the negative of a picture you would take with your camera. In a negative the colors are reversed: the areas that will print black are clear, and the areas that will be white in the finished newspaper are black. The negative is placed on a light table where imperfections caused by dust, dirt, or scratches are painted over. This is called opaquing.

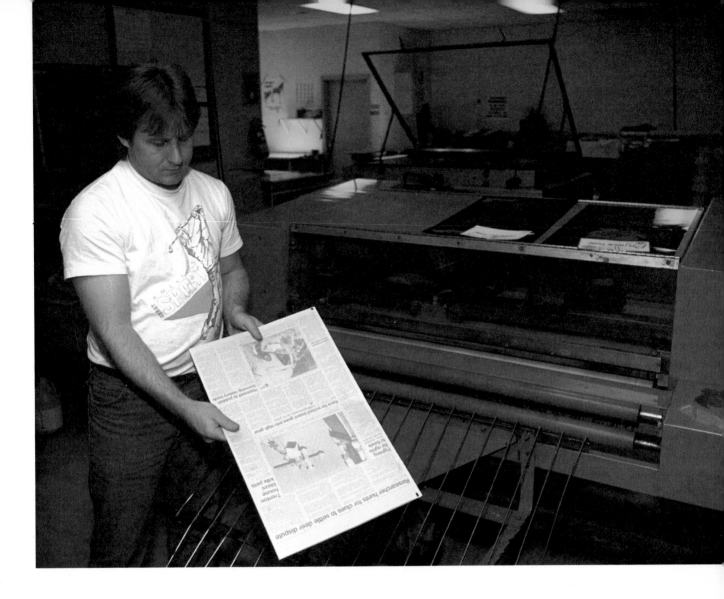

The negative is passed into a room where printing plates are made. To make each printing plate, a sheet of aluminum is fed into a machine along with the negative. Inside the machine, light passes through the clear areas of the negative and falls on a special light-sensitive coating on the aluminum. This makes an image appear on the surface of the aluminum plate.

The aluminum plates are then fastened around cylinders in the printing press. When ink is applied to the plates, Yvette's story is actually printed onto paper. The pressroom workers check the first samples off press to make sure that the printed newspapers are clear and readable. The color photographs are also checked closely to see that the colors are not too dark or too bright.

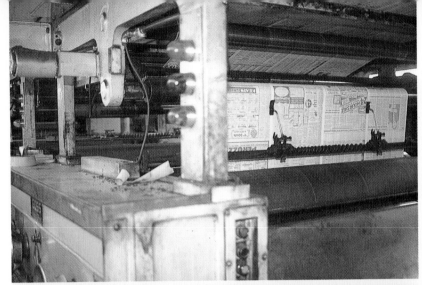

After the quality of the printing is checked, the presses feed continuous sheets of newsprint into machines that cut, fold, and combine the pages in order. A conveyor belt carries bundles of newspapers to waiting trucks for delivery. Yvette, who stayed late to work on another assignment, looks over her story in one of the first copies off the presses.

Being a newspaper reporter takes long hours of hard work—researching, interviewing, observing, and writing quickly to meet deadlines. Yvette never knows where the next story will take her, and she likes that aspect of her job best of all... because she knows that tomorrow will be another adventure.